Almajiri
A New African Poetry

Abdul-Rasheed Na'Allah

Africa World Press, Inc.

P.O. Box 1892
Trenton, NJ 08607

P.O. Box 48
Asmara, ERITREA

Africa World Press, Inc.

P.O. Box 1892
Trenton, NJ 08607

P.O. Box 48
Asmara, ERITREA

Copyright © 2001 Abdul-Rasheed Na'Allah

First Printing 2001

Cover design: Debbie Hird

Library of Congress Cataloging-in-Publication Data

Almajiri / [compiled by] Abdul-Rasheed Na'Allah
      p.   cm.
   English, Yoruba, Fula and Hausa
   ISBN 0-86543-787-4 – ISBN 0-86543-788-2 (pbk.)
   1. Street poetry, Nigerian. I. Na'Allah, Abdul-Rasheed.
 PL8014.N62A45 1999
 821–dc21   99-3145
                                                            CIP

For three women:
Saratu, Rahmat and Bilikisu

CONTENTS

Environmental & Human Exploitations

Kuzo, Let's Talk Hausa, Yoruba

Tributes, Hopes, Life

Acknowledgements

A big gratitude to my friend, Sanjit Bakshi, and his darling wife, Amritha, for their wonderful support while I was putting this poetry volume together; especially to Sanjit for type-setting it. Many other friends deserve commendations for their help: Paul, Mona, Fari, Anna, Sue, and many others who invited me at different times to perform during their public events, and thus created for me occasions to bring new poems to life. My family is always a source of strength, so thanks darling Rahmat, and dearest daughter, Saara.

I am especially grateful to Felix Mnthali, Douglas Killam, Peter Stummer and Ato Quayson for taking time to review the poems, and for their very useful comments.

Oh Allah, thanks always!

ABDUL-RASHEED NA'ALLAH,
EDMONTON,
JULY 1998

Foreword &

Introduction

Foreword

Nigeria has always been the heart of artistic, cultural and intellectual productivity in Africa and no Nigerian will even dare to show you his or her work unless it is really good. It is therefore an honour to be asked to say a few words on a fine achievement like *Almajiri*. I came to this work looking for all the usual tell-tale signs of anger, fatigue, disillusionment and horror that readers seem to have been trained to find in any work basing itself on Africa. What I found was a lyrical beauty whose power lies in a deep love for Nigeria and for Africa and whose expression is best summed up in the description of human life as a paradox. The paradox in the condition of Africa leads the poet to other instances of the human condition and extends the range of concerns that the poet's conscience covers. There are poems here on east Timor and on multinational companies as well as on dictators like Mobutu Seseseko and those thugs who gunned down Kudiratu the wife of Moshood Abiola. There is the inevitable Mandela poem. There is even a praise poem on Sir Ketumile Masire the recently retired former President of Botswana. That poem allows the author to celebrate the work of some of our other leaders such as Senghor, Nyerere and Kaunda. There is a poem on Queen Amina of Zazzau as well as on Amos Tutuola.

Real love is critical and real love stings as it caresses and caresses as it stings. That is why we find the poet lamenting Nigeria's woes which are also those of the rest of the continent in these strains from "After the Drought":

I never thought that when rain finally came,
You'd select only a few mouths for drinking.
I never thought that you could shatter
      your newly acquired glass house,
and leave its particle on the ground
for those barefooted to step on.

The discourse on the condition of Africa will often demand that those who engage in it go into the fray with no holds barred. That is a writer's privilege. It is also his or her act of faith and his or her ironic voice of love. That is why the controlling paradox in *Almajiri* immediately hit a responsive chord in me. I can relate to the pain that it invokes and the hidden joys that it celebrates. I have been there. I am there. I will always be there. So will millions of fellow Africans at home and abroad. A poem such as "After the Drought" with which *Almajiri* opens speaks to Nigeria as easily and as aptly as it speaks to Malawi, to Kenya, to Zimbabwe, or indeed, to any other country in Africa. The pain of looking at Nigeria being devoured piece by piece by a ruthless authoritarianism and a greedy elite becomes the pain of looking at a repetition of similar ravages of the plague maiming and decimating the rest of the continent. Conversely, the strength one gathers from the resilience of ordinary men, women and children in all these countries becomes the back-bone of that hope which all of us have for our beloved continent. It is a hope often betrayed by those who should know, those to whom more was given but who now put the continent up for sale in "Dan Marakantar Bokoko—The Nigerian School Goer":

> The Peacock often boasts:
> "I'm the king of birds"!
> King, kickbacking kickfronting,
> Kicking to gutter rising rays of people's hearts,
> King hawker of home treasures
> on the streets of Switzerland.

The resilience of Africa's people is like Achebe's "anthills of the savannah" always there, always watching, and, above all, always witnessing the good and the bad that is done in Africa's name:

> Haven't you seen,
> that the ocean flows without waiting for ships,
> the air blows without waiting for planes,
> the road winds without waiting for wheels,

no matter how you run, in front you will
    meet the ground!

                        ("Dan Marakantar")

Africa is patient and loving and waiting. It remains the source of peace, of hope, of rebirth and of more resilience. It is like a mother who knows what her child needs and the poet asks Africa to lure him.

into a deep sleep
so that when I wake up, afresh
I'll sing loud,
laugh from the feeling of health and peace
of a new energy.

                             ("Africa")

Here lies that paradox with which these few words began. Until things really change Africa remains the great paradox of our time. This is the continent with all the raw materials that the world needs and yet it remains the one whose people remain among the poorest on earth. In Africa itself, Nigeria exemplifies that great paradox. No country in Africa is as well endowed with raw materials, with thinkers and writers of world stature and with great universities as this giant and yet few countries on the continent have subjected their people to so much suffering. That is why voices like the one we hear in *Almajiri* remain so vital to the future of the whole continent of Africa. Such voices are like the ants in the central poem of this collection:

Ants continue to smile,
and remain proud in being *Almajirai:*
If only bullies open their ears,
if their eyes' stomachs are sensitive to their eyes,
and can can digest a meal of life,
our meal they'll ask to eat.

FELIX MNTHALI,
GABORONE, BOTSWANA,
ASCENSION DAY,
MAY 21, 1998

Introduction: Almajiri and the Songs of Street Poets

Almajiri is a common word used in Hausa, Fulani and some Yoruba communities of Nigeria, to refer to public beggars, often blind, crippled, or both. The Yoruba pronounce it as *alumajiri* because the Yoruba language[1] does not allow for consonant clusters. However, it is unlikely that this word originated from any one of these three languages. Even the Arabic language that shares morphological characteristics with *almajiri* (*al-majiri*) does not have the exact word in its vocabulary. A few Arabic words however come close to it, but have meanings different from *al-majiri*. For example, *Jara* in Arabic means "run." *Majra* means "a path" or "a channel" such as the one followed by flowing water, or by moon orbiting the earth.

The Nigerian *almajiri* has other meanings, "Quranic or Islamic school pupils." This *almajiri* is of two types: pupils who learn from relatives or from family friends as Islamic/Quranic teachers[2]. The second type consists of pupils whose parents have no prior family relationship to the teachers. Usually this category of *almajiri* suffers most because the teacher is unable to provide for them and they have to go out to beg for their own sustenance. In some circumstances, an *Almajiri*, in all the categories, begs for food for themselves as well as for their teachers.

The *Almajiri*[3] in all the instances, is also a poet. As he goes around houses and compounds begging for food, he sings to entertain his patrons and patronesses. He vocalizes out his frustration about the society and questions the system that sentences him to eat left-overs and casts him into the gutter. He asks whether it is a crime to pursue knowledge, and why a young person who wants to know more about God and his society becomes a destitute among his own people.

In Nigeria, the cry by the media, the elites and the rulers is about how the *Almajiri* becomes an easy recruit for street gangs and elements who want to revenge against the society. Nobody has ever asked if the society is fair to the *Almajiri*. There are several *God's Bits of Woods*'[4] Maïmouna in Nigeria, blind outward but who are clearly people of great vision and unequaled courage inward, who daily convey their messages to the society in their songs and chants, but to whom no one listens.

I do not think any Nigerian or indeed African better qualifies to call him or herself a poet than the *Almajiri*. He walks through all corners of the community, listening to lamentations of families that are unable to cloth or feed their babies and who, along with their children, die slowly from hunger and disease. He knows the neighbor who just yesterday rode bicycle to the office but who today after becoming a government minister put up a gigantic building blocking paths where neighbors walk daily.

Unfortunately, nobody wants to hear his songs, except the poor, who constitute the majority of his patrons. *Almajiri* is an eye sore, a parasite to the Nigerian elite, who knock him down on numerous occasions with their cars.

I have chosen to call this anthology *Almajiri* partly to air the voices of all these beggars. Beyond that however, I am also an *Almajiri*[5]. Twice in Ilorin as a young boy I lived with my Father's friends as a Quranic/Islamic pupil. I was lucky however to be minimally fed and clothed, to the extent the teachers could afford. In one of the instances, one of my teacher's sons was also an *Almajiri* with my Father. However unlike me, he did not have to share with tens of other kids but only with my brother, born directly after me, who was much younger than him[6].

With Niyi Osundare's poems I learnt that modern African poetry written in English can be as simple and as accessible to the ordinary readers or listeners as the *Almajiri* songs are to those who listen to them. My undergraduate literature teachers[7] convinced me that poems in English do not have to be esoteric. Discussing Osundare's poems with Russ Chambers, an American, who despite being a native speaker of English[8] became obsessed with the magic of simplicity in "Art is an Ass," opened my eyes beyond the mysticism of high school days. I realized at that point that poems written in English can be blended with traditional African flavor, and that English, an elitist language, can be explored to represent issues that concern the common person. I performed many modern African poems on Sokoto television (NTV Sokoto, based in Sokoto city) in the late 1970s[9], but never at any of those times felt that I was engaging in a conversation with the Nigerian audience. The Sokoto State Government built television centers in many corners of the Sokoto city and the common people could gather there to watch. Whenever I returned home from the college for the end of term break many would say they saw me on television, but none told me they understood what I was saying. In most instances, I didn't either. Even when we accompanied the poems with Yoruba or Hausa songs and danced and memorized them word for word, we easily realized that what we danced to and really enjoyed were the songs rather that the esoteric lines. Although some of those poems were politically charged, there was no way their messages could reach the audience made up largely of Nigerians who either never or barely attended Western schools. One day a student colleague of mine told me bluntly that each time we went on stage he always thought we went temporarily mad.

I have engaged in a few polemics about how not to be an elitist in contemporary African writing because elitism in modern Africa means alienation from the population[10]. The poems in this collection represent a blend of African and English cultures, and what I hope will be accessible to a local literate Nigerian and African audience. For those who cannot understand English, but speak Hausa or Yoruba, I hope the refrains will rekindle their experiences which I have tried to capture in the poems. I have written elsewhere[11] that African writers should prepare to use both foreign and indigenous languages in their writings. The poems in Hausa and Yoruba are, for me, an attempt to continue to show that contemporary African writers in European languages would benefit African communities more if they write as well in local African tongues. I have retained the Ilorin and Sokoto dialects of Yoruba and Hausa languages respectively in my poetry because I do not subscribe to the idea that a writer needs to produce his works in the so-called standard dialect. This, afterall, is creativity, and the whole concept of standardization kills literary and aesthetic identity of every work of art.

Most of the poems in *Almajiri* come alive in actual performance where their socio-cultural and literary aesthetics are fully realized. I have recommended performance elements needed for some of the poems and allowed every performer to explore personal initiatives for others. My attempt here is to continue the vibrant tradition of a wonderful generation of Nigerian poets, Osundare, Tanure Ojaide, Okinba Launko, etc., who explore folktales and several oral performance forms in a creativity that remain fresh and accessible to the audience.

ABDUL-RASHEED NA'ALLAH
EDMONTON, DECEMBER 1997

Introduction Notes

1   The Yoruba word for "beggar" is *onibara* or *alubara*.
    The Yoruba saying, *oni bara nb'ole bo*, means "the beg-
    gar is starting to behave like a thief." But the root
    word, *bara*, is also in the Hausa language. *Bara* in
    Hausa, like in Yoruba, means begging. "Za ni je bara"
    in Hausa means, "I shall go begging [on the street,
    etc].

2   In this case the *Almajiri* are like children to their
    teachers and are expected to be treated with the same
    love and care that the teachers would give their own
    biological children.

3   The woman beggar will be *almajira* in Hausa; plural
    almajirai. However, the Yoruba wouldn't make such a
    distinction because gender and number are not
    marked in Yoruba language through affixations. It
    will most likely be "*alumajiri okunrin*, a man beggar,"
    and *alumajiri obinrin*, a woman beggar, and *awon
    alumajiri*, beggars.

4   Sembene Ousmane in *God's Bits of Wood* and, espe-
    cially, Mariama Bâ in *The Beggar's Strike*, are examples
    Senegalese writers who confront these sociopolitical
    situations of beggars in their own communities.

5   I started elementary one (Primary 1) as an *Almajiri*
    and continued until well after primary four before I
    moved to live with my father where I continued to

learn the Quran and a few other Islamic knowledge books written in Arabic.

6   My father didn't maintain a large Quranic school. Both of them were the school, except on occasions when a couple of children from the neighborhood joined them to learn the Quran and the science of Hadith.

7   I have in mind an American, Dr. Russ Chambers; an Indian, Dr. PD Tripathi; and a Ugandan, Dr. Stephen Lubega, to whom I remain grateful. Not that some African poets had not before then embedded their poems with local metaphors, especially negritude writers, and many non-negritudists from Anglo-Africa, but their works were either not often chosen for literature lessons by teachers or were written in such a way that whatever local images they included were buried under the tombs of their iron-hard expressions. In my first year at university, my Professors helped me to discover that another way existed for poetry creativity in English.

8   It never occurred to me before then that a native speaker of English would consider simple English as an asset. I had thought that complex English expression was a sign of a writer's expertise and greatness in the language.

9   As members of the Dramatic Society of Government Teachers' College (GTC), Birnin Yauri, Nigeria, one

Mr. 'Demola Araoye, our Social Studies teacher pre-pared us for poetry performances on Sokoto televi-sion. We also performed at the college hall. Birnin Yauri was a boarding college, and was over three hun-dred kilometers away from Sokoto city.

10 See my articles, "Arts and Revolution in Africa," *The Punch*. 15 January 1986, p. 9.; "The Africanness of African Poetry," *The Punch*. 7 February, 1987, p. 10+ (6 Instalments); "Wole Soyinka: Neither Readable Nor Popular," *New Nigeria*. 28 March, 1988, p. 20; "Artist, Commitment and the Popular Audience: A Challenge of A New Decade," *Bedrock*. 3.3, 1991, pp. 40–4.

11 See the sub-section, "Issues Germane to African Literature in the Twenty-First Century," pp. 571–9, in my paper, "African Literatures and Postcolonialism: Projections into the Twenty-First Century." *Canadian Review of Comparative Literature*. 22.3–4, 1995, pp. 569–85.

Issues

After the Drought. . .

After the drought that dug
for you a thousand graves,
after the dryness that made your land search for tears,
but ended up shedding blood from its eyes,
after the collective murder of your humanity,
I never thought that when rain finally came,
You'd select only a few mouths for drinking.
I never thought that you could shatter your newly
acquired glass house,
and leave its particles on the ground
for those barefooted to step on.

I never thought that you could wash your dirty hands
shamelessly on the street, and take
from our mother the pride she had of her labor.
I never thought you could murder her hope,
and render moot her maternal pains.

Nights, days she couldn't sleep,
she couldn't stand without considering
what her baby felt.
Never wanted a stillborn!
Some nights, she turned, turned, re-turned
wanting her child to have peace,
even if she herself was in pain.

That pain was sweet to her,
as long as her kid was kicking.

Ungrateful pigs!
Would you have food,
If this mother hadn't farmed!
Yet, She mustn't feed,
from the crops she plucked.
No, she mustn't drink
from the water she helped to draw,
Hún-ùn, she mustn't enjoy the free ray of the sun!

Mother!
Keep on smiling, mother.
Their blind bulbs can't see the forming cloud,
their sightless eyes can't see that
    no matter how vigorously
they wash their filthy hands on you,
Your impervious clothes wouldn't let their dirt taste
    your skin.
When the new rain thus drop,
it'll be smooth, mother.
You'll drink, and all your children
Will drink.

Tabarmar kunya –
the Mat of Shame

Sun shimfida tabarmar kunya
Duk duniya
Sun bar mu kwan bisa
Har dariyar mu suke
'Yar duniya

My orifice, a home
to thousand tales
Bees bearing pots of honey
for the world to drink.
Oh chorus friends, this song of bees.

Sun shimfida tabarmar kunya
Duk duniya
Sun bar mu kwan bisa
Har dariyar mu suke
'Yar duniya

My songs, yet
Bakaken Amurka,
My Hausa thinks of you:
"Kwanta ka mutu,
Ka ga mai kaunar ka":
Pretend to be dead, and see who loves you.

Sun shimfida tabarmar kunya
Duk duniya
Sun bar mu kwan bisa
Har dariyar mu suke
'Yar duniya

My songs,
"Gaskiyar ta fi kwabo,"
Truth, worth more than dala[1].
The sun rises early and swallows
the thread of darkness on the sky.
The moon swims in the ocean of shiny water
splashing shining tides on the ground.
Oh, who'll swim with me in this water
 and be robed in the garment of truthful light!

Sun shimfida tabarmar kunya
Duk duniya
Sun bar mu kwan bisa
Har dariyar mu suke
'Yar duniya

---

1 This is the currency American dollar in Hausa, mean-
 ing here one dollar. However the idea is just the
 money, could be thousands or millions of dollars.

32

The sun rises early
to break the darkly day.
The moon shines at night
to light the sleeping night.

The sun, the moon, have hearts of light,
A thousand fingers cannot cover their lights.
Your hearts, folks
Your only *gaskiyar to fi kwabo*[2].

> *Sun shimfida tabarmar kunya*
> *Duk duniya*
> *Sun bar mu kwan bisa*
> *Har dariyar mu suke*
> *'Yar duniya*

Our village ballad
sets our feet early on the ground
with his salty songs,
"Let your souls touch your hearts," sings he,
"As you forge on today."

---

2 The Hausa adage, "Thruth is more than money,"
   Kwabo actually is the Nigerian money which used to
   be greater than the American one dollar up till the
   late 70s to the early 80s. There is a Nigerian Hausa
   newspaper called "Gaskiyar ta fi kwabo".

Sun shimfida tabarmar kunya
Duk duniya
Sun bar mu kwan bisa
Har dariyar mu suke
'Yar duniya

The ballad's titillating voice
abiding in our ears,
"Birds' desires to ride into the sky,
Fuel their feathers' navigation beyond the earth."

Sun shimfida tabarmar kunya
Duk duniya
Sun bar mu kwan bisa
Har dariyar mu suke
'Yar duniya

When birds fly
Their feathers push air backward.
A swimmer reaches the coast
By pushing water backward.
A day breaks,
By pushing night backward.
Our bees must open their pots of honey,
and push backward their voracious poison!

Sun shimfida tabarmar kunya
Duk duniya
Sun bar mu kwan bisa
Har dariyar mu suke
'Yar duniya

Our moons and suns
must show their lights.
Our birds
Must use their feathers to climb
deep into the sky!

Sun shimfida tabarmar kunya
Duk duniya
Sun bar mu kwan bisa
Har dariyar mu suke
'Yar duniya

Baƙaken Amurka,
These bushes invaded with flies,
these ghettos must clear
to the breeze of lingering freshness of a scent-full air.
Our eyes deserve food that gives pleasure to their fas-
tened household,
Our legs should walk on the gold of our new floor,
Our heads should lay on these diamond beds!

Sun shimfida tabarmar kunya
Duk duniya
Sun bar mu kwan bisa
Har dariyar mu suke
'Yar duniya

The *tabarmar kunya* they spread
for us
shall be their mats to sleep!

Sun shimfida tabarmar kunya
Duk duniya
Sun bar mu kwan bisa
Har dariyar mu suke
'Yar duniya

Oh,
What a world with a mat of shame!
What a person sleeps on it!
If they make the mat, you tear the mat!!

Sun shimfida tabarmar kunya
Duk duniya
Sun bar mu kwan bisa
Har dariyar mu suke
'Yar duniya!

36

Poco

Talk to me my friend,
If you know how to talk.
The tortoise isn't a stranger to the farmer;
the farmer caught him more than once
    plucking his crops.
The listener isn't a stranger to words;
more than once he outwitted words, breaking words
    into pieces.
Talk, it's the food for the person who hears.

Tongues gyrate in the gymnastics of mouth
Only a tongue looking for shame
goes outside the mouth to exercise its muscles.
The day the eyes underrated the sun,
that day the eyes went home and never returned.
The day legs underrated Alberta snow,
and walked the town naked in a dead December,
it's doubtful if those legs ever returned.

Poco,
No, I'm not asking your amplifier not to boom.
Only,
when your hunter wants a round in the Yankari forest,
let him pay homage to the forest's spirits,
let him learn how to swim in the ocean of the forest's
    thickness.

Sing along, my song

(To be performed with an accompaniment of a music from the African talking drum, in the rhythms of the wordings of the refrain)

Refrain: *Ika owo kan ko le mu*
　　　　　Ika owo kan ko le mu
　　　　　Reluwe duro oo

Sallama,
my feathers navigate
from the shore of my sunny hills.
Forecomers,
Eagle, King of birds
bids you salutations
with the juiciest tongue
of our forefathers' seasongs.
Bids,
sing along, my song;
bids to invoke your ancestry,
Our heritage, shoulder-to-shoulder.

　　　　　Ika owo kan ko le mu
　　　　　Ika owo kan ko le mu
　　　　　Reluwe duro oo

Sing along, my song,
a summon for our common rise.
Africans of the Northern snow!
Sing, this song must
Refresh your flesh
for the booming blood
—of our unity.
For our profit, in these choosy
markets of our common miseries.

> *Ika owo kan ko le mu*
> *Ika owo kan ko le mu*
> *Reluwe duro oo*

Kins,
my colorful songs draw no lines.
Come, people, come,
Dance to the cause
for the demise of
gutter homelands, garbage counties of America.
Dance to the tune
Peak-calling the African American birds to
Compete in a battle of our world.

> *Ika owo kan ko le mu*
> *Ika owo kan ko le mu*
> *Reluwe duro oo*

A finger
Hasn't the chest to touch
the moving car;
Can it then attempt
To stop the running train!
Kins,
Let my songs cry aloud
in your souls.

> *Ika owo kan ko le mu*
> *Ika owo kan ko le mu*
> *Reluwe duro oo*

I see
Snowland Africans' flowers
to harmful walls,
Instead of chemicals,
crushing them to the ground.
African-American Jordans!
Billion pocketed lawyers,
Magnets of New York Markets:
Frustrate the million walls of the hate-mongers.
These gutters, these homelands
Seek your might to
End their miseries.
How can the giraffe store food in his home,
Yet cry that his mother's children are dying of hunger!

Ika owo kan ko le mu
Ika owo kan ko le mu
Reluwe duro oo

Small indeed is the needle,
No Cock can swallow it as food.
Your joint-fingers can
lift the over beaten iron-sheets
And turn the American homelands
Into American Cambridge!
Sing, sing along,
my song.

Ika owo kan ko le mu
Ika owo kan ko le mu
Reluwe duro oo

* The refrain, written in Yoruba, means "A finger cannot stop/hold down the moving train."

Dan Makarantar Bokoko— the Nigerian School Goer

(To be accompanied by rhythmic clapping of hands)

Lead: *Dan Makaranta bokoko*
         Ba karatu ba sallah
         Sai yawan ɓaci Malam

Refrain: *Dan Makanra bokoko*
          Ba karatu ba sallah
          Sai yawan ɓaci Malam

The Nigerian Peacock
Prides himself on going to school.
Ties his neck with a swinging rope.
Hands in his pockets,
Swears at Malam, at own mother and father
Swears at Qur'an
Forehead unbowed to the ground.

         Dan Makaranta bokoko
         Ba karatu ba sallah
         Sai yawan ɓaci Malam

Our verse for the Nigerian Peacock!
Elegant in outer robes,
Water of sewage kind oceans his inner stomach:
When he spits
Militant odor homes the street;
Dan Makaranta bokoko!

> *Dan makaranta bokoko*
> *Ba karatu ba sallah*
> *Sai yawan ɓaci Malam*

The Peacock often boasts:
"I'm the king of birds"!
King, kickbacking kickfronting,
Kicking to gutter rising rays of people's hearts,
King hawker of home treasures on the streets of
    Switzerland.

> *Dan makaranta bokoko*
> *Ba karatu ba sallah*
> *Sai yawan ɓaci Malam*

Dan Makaranta bokoko
his science does not go to the sky
his arts know no angle to draw
but yet a wizard he is,
erecting a gigantic house with saliva
soon his building shall be bulldozed by ants.

Dan makaranta bokoko
Ba karatu ba sallah
Sai yawan ɓaci Malam

Nigerian Peacock, wizard of the night!
Haven't you seen,
that the ocean flows without waiting for ships,
the air blows without waiting for planes,
the road winds without waiting for wheels,
no matter how fast you run, in front you will
meet the ground!

Dan makaranta bokoko
Ba karatu ba sallah
Sai yawan ɓaci Malam

Pomo

If a child doubts his own birth,
the elder lends him a story from her pots of life.
She tells him that the sun
rises from the same spot it rises, sets at the same spot
    it sets,
even if he hopes otherwise and changes often
    his hopes.
Chameleon changes colors, making him chameleon;
can't change being a chameleon.

Sometime it rains, sometime it doesn't.
Cool, moistened air blows around sometime, some
    places;
Some places sometime, the air, hot and dry.
Some places it's cool all times, and hot all times in
    some.
Nature hasn't other name.

On air from Frankfurt,
I listened:
"Of course it's relative,
Who knows?"
People plenty who know,
and people as many as fishes in oceans who don't.

The rat who doubts that cat eats flesh,
better don't go near the cat,
else it'll be too late for it to know.

Many rats doubt what cats are up to,
and many give cats feasts of their own flesh!
A rat has a mind, but a rat has two minds,
What else?
Green is green, blue is blue,
If nothing blurs one's vision.
A child who isn't a magician,
and hasn't swallowed some burn-me-not herbs,
Will get burnt
if she puts her hand into fire;
What else is Truth, pomo?

Al-Ikhlas

Tori don get K leg,
za song wei zey come for broda him mouz
he be broda rait rait,
but him talk don de show
zat hin head don become kolony
fo he talk-talk dogon turenci
come get larabci add foram
him say I be *almukhlit*,
fo how I go be blaki
come take Musulumi come add
hin say africamusulumi no de fo book,
na mixcha, so him come talk-talk.

He no come stop fo zia
Hin say to be africamusulumi
na to be guilty fo kill-kill
na him bi say the kind guilty
wey once upon a time
zey come nak fo one Nobbel laureate hin nek
for him obodo kontri, na treasonbrohaha!
Za ajwaya wey be accuser,
Na him become za alkali.
Any wey, I now know
say mai babbanriga na blaki
no bi musulumi hin be,

and me wei wear am,
na *al-mukhlit*.

I know say mai uncle Bamidele
wei bi muezzin for our mosque
wei zey call in arabic with Yoruba him tongue:
"Alau aki baru!"
na *almukhlit* na him hinbi,
no need fo him fine fine mind fo salat
no need fo him *shahada* fo hin Lord
afrikamusulumi na apostates,
      na hin dis broda talk-talk.

But I get one question wey I won ask broda:
Za fishes wey de fo ocean
and za fishes wei zey fo riber
zen get different name zen zey call am?
When za sun comot fo out fo Nigeria
and za sun comot fo out fo Canada
Hin get different name zen zey call am?
Za hungry Cripples wei zey fo Rijiyan-ɗorowa
Za hungry Cripples wey zey fo Onitcha market
Zen get different name zen zey call am?

Haba 'Danbature,
wata no get enemy fa!
I be blaki, I be brawni, na person na him we all be

I be from Sierra Leone, I be from Amurka,
    na kontri na him we all get,
no one come come from sky.
Yu no kuku allow him kitab mouz talk,
wheza him zey put dabaru fo worship.

Him true name na *Al-Ikhlas*, na One Him be.
Abi you no sabi za kind One I zey talk?
Na One be say,
afrikamusulumi, arabumusulumi, amurkamusulumi,
sinomusulumi,
na Musulumi na him him be,
Kumasi, Makka, Greece, Kyoto,
all una face face Ka'aba,
all una talk na say Hin Great,
all una do na head fo ground,
whether una white, abi una blaki, ko una brawn,
abi una mix mix Larabci fo una Okrika,
Ikhlas.

The Hen has Learnt about its Game

The hen has learnt about its game
A thing of heart a thing of mind
Its mind can see beyond the corn
It knows about the push to run
It hears the pain and knows the love:
To search the filth can cause its death.

The hen has come on its kneel to talk
It eats a lot of the dirt we know
The soon the cocks of the town emerge
That soon the hen in the town it goes.

To know it's a cock black and shine
or a type with a flowing gown
Or see it's the cock silk and fine
that's the cock it'll be chasing to town.

Astagfirullah, the hen in trance!
its hands are up,
its mouth is dry.
It enjoys the game,
and detests the dirt.

Celebration,

Communality,

Human-Hood

Aramanda

In dedication to Global Education Conference,
Edmonton, 1996, and for Sue Brigham
(To the accompaniment of music from the African talking drum)

Refrain: *Ore je ka jo[1]*
          Ara je ka jo
          Ore je ka jo o
          Ore mi

Dance to this feast
of our common heritage,
a feast of our booming friendship.

        Ore je ka jo
        Ara je ka jo
        Ore je ka jo o
        Ore mi

The Sun prides itself for having eyes that see,

---

1 The refrain stanza, written in Yoruba, translates thus:
Oh friend, dance with me/Oh beloved, dance
with me/Our dance of friendship/Our dance of
life (Oh, my friend!)

West, East
It dances for the joy, that it
Brings fruits,
From the soil of our global fertility.

> *Ore je ka jo*
> *Ara je ka jo*
> *Ore je ka jo o*
> *Ore mi*

The Sun's burning eyes,
Brighten the darkness of the day
Edify the earth
Awaken the lives of our icy bodies.
Sun is one in the sky,
One is humanity.

> *Ore je ka jo*
> *Ara je ka jo*
> *Ore je ka jo o*
> *Ore mi*

The taste of cocoa water
Proves the richness of coconut.
The love for human lives
Proves the humanity in a person.

Ore je ka jo
Ara je ka jo
Ore je ka jo o
Ore mi

Cuba to Korea, Greece to Guinea-Bissau:
walls in an iron building.
Yet some dogs, human blood,
fill their mouths with human flesh.
Ogoni bullshell burnt to ashes pregnant women,
and kept aborted babies for toast
    in their Shelling meetings in London.
Jet companies, fat cows in the copperbelt ,
Confused Congolese on the streets of Kinshasha.

Ore je ka jo
Ara je ka jo
Ore je ka jo o
Ore mi

Friend, if your eyes can calculate, what number does
    this come to?:
In West African farms,
Cocoa crops multiply on ridges,
farmers, rag-lean, hanging one leg on one thigh,
As cocoa butter flowers the stalls
    of North American Safe-Way.

Ore je ka jo
Ara je ka jo
Ore je ka jo o
Ore mi

As Ogoni blood continues to flow to Britain and
    America,
London, Washington, D. C. ,
Wheels wheel on,
Wheels wheeling on blood as if running on gas.

Global village:
The pythagoras theory in this calculator
I rub your back, you cut mine to the bones:
a village for a new bondage:
Another slavery in the oven of an impending century.

Ore je ka jo
Ara je ka jo
Ore je ka jo o
Ore mi

My eyes glare for feeling species on this earth,
My hands search to tap hearts yet unlocked;
my ears, to hear the voices of those whose words spell
    love, friendship, and justice.

Ore je ka jo
Ara je ka jo
Ore je ka jo o
Ore mi

Oh grow, plant, grow!
As roses grow in Alberta soil.
Aramanda[2], your salty seed
Is the flavor for our hopeful future.

Ore je ka jo
Ara je ka jo
Ore je ka jo o
Ore mi

---

2 A Yoruba word which meanings include "a wonder of
   life"

Africa

Ilé eni ki ba'ni l'eru, wo'lé, wo'lé
Ilé eni ki ba'ni l'eru, wo'lé, wo'lé

My head knows why it leads me to your home, Africa
It knows that's where I belong.
As my head touches Ilorin soil,
it smiles aloud
for arriving safely at home.
Africa, the home of a child doesn't terrorize the child!

Ilé eni ki ba'ni l'eru, wo'lé, wo'lé
Ilé eni ki ba'ni l'eru, wo'lé, wo'lé

Africa, my toes are hungry for a journey across the
Sahara,
I want to drink from the sweet water of your Congo
rivers,
and swim from Ethiopia to Egypt,
Africa, I want a taste of your un-polluted crops,
Your Mangoes and Nuts,
Your Oranges and Guava.

Ilé eni ki ba'ni l'eru, wo'lé, wo'lé
Ilé eni ki ba'ni l'eru, wo'lé, wo'lé

Breathe your peace into me, Africa,
Robe me in your smooth arms.
My restless soul wants your warmth,
to comfort the sleepless eyes of its body,
Lure me into a deep sleep
so that when I wake up, afresh
I'll sing aloud,
and laugh from the feeling of health and peace,
from the eagerness of a new energy.

> *Ilé eni ki ba'ni l'eru, wolé, wolé*
> *Ilé eni ki ba'ni l'eru, wolé, wolé*

Africa
Let the world hear your rhythm,
even if they often compromise your life.
It's time, Africa
to spread your abundance arm
and show the amazing wealth
of your strength.

> *Ilé eni ki ba'ni l'eru, wolé, wolé*
> *Ilé eni ki ba'ni l'eru, wolé, wolé*

Africa,
Drag on no longer your feet,
This millennium that begs to visit your warmth,

Must know how well you deserve his visit.
Come out Africa,
Spread your arms,
Put your glittering diamonds,
beyond the cyberspace.

African Biscuit

Teeth smile when they sense an
impending appointment with you,
saliva takes to the street,
when it smells the fragrance of
your flavor.
African biscuit,
you're in a cult with *koko, kunu, gari* and *eko-gbona*,
African biscuit, unequaled in the theater of flavor.

Kraakakaka, Krakaka,
    You make sound so sweet to our teeth's ears,
The teeth builds a smooth street for you.
    Your aroma makes the nose dance
    all through the night,
praying for the day to break,
so that she can be the first to tap on your door.
Your redolence makes the mouth swear
that you're the best friend he has.

Oh, these nuts of our ground,
generous with oil to help our soup,
a friend to pepper, a friend to salt,
though flowing on the grinding stone,
stands strong in its hut of pan.
When you walk out from your hut, *kuli kuli*

We're always on hand to celebrate your coming.
African biscuit,
your response is like no other in town.

Gratitude-Godiya

Godiya,
Teacher by the pen:
My ink is naught
But for Command, be,
and it is
Pouring on paper as a witch pours out her
undoing in the market square.

Oh,
Not me to chose this voice.
You gave't t'me, and
Asked, be audible
to the deafest demons in the forest!
Once Thou will
who unwills!

Earthbird!
Sing again
Strike the gutter
With your Staff of words
Strike hard
With your razor pen
Strike the stinking sewage back
at the faces of its gatherers.
. Maᵭaukakin Sarki,

these teeth you gave
to our hawks
they use
to massacre chicks in the household,
they drink their blood
and drink
Drink as if drinking water gushing from Olumoh
        spring.

Godiya,
my pen's teeth
Will war to its ink's last drop.
My Alfa's voices
ring in my pens' ears:
Do not dose off
when hawks eat off
the flesh
of their kin.

Oh,
when would they feel
the beating of their hearts!
When would these lizards
know that the walls they mount to the top
were Your construction, oh Ubangiji!
Godiya, this Staff will stuff their ears
with your words.

Squirrel

I lifted my hand to sweep you off the ground, squirrel,
but found that the wind had
blown you away from me.
Tokyo Squirrel,
the wind carried you high
so high into the Austin sea.

I never thought my graphic words
would dance away
so easily from your eyes
I never knew that the wind would
chase out through your
    left ear
the golden signals
    I inserted deep into your right ear.
Squirrel,
I never thought my deafening drumbeats
were so muted in your ears:
so still you sat,
instead of taking to the floor
of my festive altar.

Tender Squirrel,
Your eyeballs performed the magic
that leaves my hearts open
Your slowly flowing words

entered the softer veins of my skin
Your angelic smile brightened, overwhelmed my eyes.

As you raised your head
and looked up into my anxious cores,
I fell flat to your loving feet
asking your hairy chest to meet mine on the grass,
asking for us to swim along the flowering bliss of the
      morning.

Yet youthful Squirrel,
     you went off with the wind,
and grew wings, navigating across the Austin waters,
you surrendered
to the tides of the China ocean.

Still Squirrel
 a piece of your eyelid,
is safely kept in the wallet of my heart.
I'll be there
at Heavenly Peace Gate[1] to return the lid to its family
I'll come
to receive you in my arms
and take you to the elysian fields
of Sobi Hill.

---

1 "Heavenly Peace Gate" is the meaning in English of
  Tiananmen, a popular Square in China.

Environmental,

Human Exploitation

Kuluso

(to the accompaniments of hand-clapping and or
African talking drum)

In dedication to the APEC Counter-Conference in
Edmonton, and to Annahid and Fariba

> Kulusọ[1]
> Abiyamọ f'ẹyin sọ
> Kulusọ
> Abiyamọ f'ẹyin sọ

My grandmother
Tells me stories
about kuluso,
the tiny king of the inner-sand,
about Liili,
the dancing-lord of the under-rock.

---

1 *Kuluso*, *Liili* are animals (*kuluso* is perhaps better
described as an insect) found mostly in sand and
rocks respectively, both are especially common in the
tropics. This song, in Yoruba, is among the popular
songs we sang as kids during children's games.

Kulusọ
Abiyamọ f'ẹyin sọ
Kulusọ
Abiyamọ f'ẹyin sọ

Liili,
Swinging its body around
  the hairy paths of rocky hills
Breathing light-sweet breeze of an un-polluted space
Eating and drinking in the
  un-ruptured sea of nature
Liili, a smiling child of the under-rock

Kulusọ
Abiyamọ f'ẹyin sọ
Kulusọ
Abiyamọ f'ẹyin sọ

Kulusọ,
Your innocent smiles
were in harmony with the whistles of your homely
  rocks
Your smiles synthesize with the sonorous melody of
  the singing birds,
and the yawning sounds of the well-fed lizards
  heading home for a nap

Your smiles speak with the laughter of the sea that
          shows its teeth as it jumps up in an ecstasy of
          happiness

Kulusǫ, your calm world suites the inner rhythms of the
offspring of the inner-sand

          Kulusǫ
          Abiyamǫ f'ęyin sǫ
          Kulusǫ
          Abiyamǫ f'ęyin sǫ

Kulusǫ, how come you run away when these souls
          sing your name?
How come, as liili, you take to your heels and run
          inside the sand?
You deem your eyes in suspicion of the singers:
Human rights? None.
Only "humans" have rights!
Earth, Oceans, Fishes, Lizards, have no rights,
just goods to be looted in day light!
No, you've no rights!
Only energy to be confiscated by night marauders
          who converge to share their loot,
No rights, not one: only deaths, and
tears from the suffocating eyes of your dying
          atmosphere!

Kulusọ
Abiyamọ f'ẹyin sọ
Kulusọ
Abiyamọ f'ẹyin sọ

Liili, you wrote no letter to invite brutes to rupture the
        harmony of your world:
or rogues to steal from you the calm of your body,
to mute the songs once so loud,
to cut the throats of the singing birds:
        leaving a broken voice of an un-relented avis!
Oh,
The lizard's stomach is cut open
The rocks broken, the sea destroyed,
the earth's womb uprooted by the greedy ghosts
        looking to assuage their palms.
Liili, the under-rock baby cries un-end from the pain of
its agony:

Kulusọ
Abiyamọ f'ẹyin sọ
Kulusọ
Abiyamọ f'ẹyin sọ

Kulusọ, Liili, my bitter words to the looters of your
        power

whose bulbs bloom stolen energy from the arrested
        river:

     "That globe that lights your world, and gives
          life to your tamed gadgets,
     That globe that rotates around your sphere,
     Shall Break, and the global village may return to
          darkness!
     Except you restore this world to the state of its
     origin, and allow it its share of its stolen earth."

Liili, soon, they'll cry, and will get no one to pet them,
trust me, Kulusọ!

        Kulusọ
        Abiyamọ f'ẹyin sọ
        Kulusọ
        Abiyamọ f'ẹyin sọ

East Timor's Tremor

(for the two East Timorian Women who opened their
pains in public)

Tremor in Timor!
East Timor's tremor,
Tremulous Timor,
from the chief anesthesia
of Indo-n- asia.

Ever had a headache?
And felt some tremor,
and felt your neck off?
That's child's play
in Timor's tremor!

Timor can't have a head,
can't have a mouth,
they can't have necks,
only blinded eyes
on tremored shoulders.

My eyes run heavy,
hearing this tale
of how immaculate maids

lose their bodies
in tremulous Timor.

Ever heard that women
had their bodies ripped off,
in open light?
That's child's play
in tremulous Timor.

No ease in East Timor,
occupant soldiers,
occupy their plants,
suck their nectars
throw emptied cells
to rot in gutter.

Birds of a feather
flock together.
Hawks in town for a feast:
Anesthesia of Indo-n-asia,
and kids of his feather,
drinking their liquor,
while East Timor,
dying in tremor.

Pens and Pencils,
Carry your papers,
Take your posters,
End the tremor!

Multinational Companies

Alarm!
The earth shouts 'alarm'!
and cries for the Shellock to spare its life.
The earth's eyes
Sore from the cry of pain
meted out by the daggers of the Shellock of death!

What's this game,
this raw mongering being played
on the earth of our lands!
Another slavery
by the giant traders
of death.

Multinational Companies!
They'll draw away the water left
for us to drink.
Their pipes are ready,
Their planes, their ships,
Their Stealths[1] ,
To Sardine our food away,
And bomb whoever obstructs their way.

---

1 American fighter planes that fly without being
   noticed and drop bombs on their targets.

Seseseko Fire

Did you see Seseseko fire,
which fiercely burnt our grasses, destroyed our crops,
    and the trees
that held our land firm from eroding?
Did you see when it burnt our huts and houses,
and sent us out naked to the galleys of gaseous lakes?
Did you see when Seseseko fire chopped off
our fingers and dumped them in the flowing river!

Did you not see how Seseseko fire
choked us with smelly flames and flurry smoke;
our eyes cried cries of painful pain, our mouths
    suffered imprisonment
at the hands of Filching Leopard,
our heads died deaths unknown before to our
    herbalists,
Seseseko fire's hands of death broke new ground
in their mastery of silent wasting.

Who would wonder at the expertise
of a Tsetse fly and a Seseseko fire!
No, you're not just a flamer, Seseseko,
you mastered your art from the sorcerer of open
    burning,

You schemed the schemes of your Tsetse fly sorcerer,
and killed our cows,
our grasses,
You snatched our fowls from us,
You cut our vegetables,
and ran away with them to the open market of your
Tsetse fly.

Oh Sesek fire, Kinshasha to Cairo!
Sesek fire, Oh!
When will you see
that your fire's burnt out!

Almajiri

Ants walk the village paths, innocently,
searching for larva and lore,
sniffing, touching, looking to see
how the sun rises and sets.
Almajiri, the ants cry for a chance to grow;
but meet death from the bullet feet of citybullers.

Ants eat leftovers and smile at the chance to feed,
but bullies condemn ants as worms of chance.
Alas, ants fall on their faces, kneel, prostrate
to have leftovers to eat,
yet smile
at the chance to feed.

Palm-patterns come in different shapes,
and tread different directions on the palm:
Palm-patterns know that many roads lead to the
        market.
Citybullies block their own ears,
whenever their palms want to talk to them.
Almajiri must wear our garments
or wear no garments,
or face the courts!

Ants continue to smile,
and remain proud in being *Almajirai*:
If only bullies open their ears,
if their eyes stomachs are sensitive to their eyes,
and can digest a meal of life,
our songs-meal they'll ask to eat.

Crumble Rumble

Click!
Complicated composure.
Compunction? Not this century!
Conbrio conceit, concretizing concubinage.
Claqueur Councilor.
Clandestine clairvoyant!

Coincidence?
Kinkajou cohabitation.
Kola,
Cancer corroding country.
Konkobility,
Caressing no kipper, kill.
Kittle crookery! ❧

Crazy crook!
Kerosened, keratosed county,
Crippled country.

Kudiratu

"Ina lillahi wa inna ilaehi raajihun,"
I uttered, recovering
from the news that you were gunned down,
right in your car!

Kudiratu,
I never did recover,
Angry questions, rocketing my mind:
When did Nigeria become a hunting reserve?
When did hunters begin to hunt
for human lives?
When did hunters mark you as prey!

Kudiratu,
I now know how low
    our roof has come.
I know that the owners of this rotting house,
Cannot snore on for long.
The coldest sound ever to enter your chest,
The electric cold that overpowered our own chests,
Must wake the owners up,
and push them to take back,
their house!

This Night...

This night I seek my sight.
This night, I seek my feeling,
I seek that which is might.

Today I have a calling
Today, I have a sight,
I have that which is grilling!

I seek you, my flesh.
I seek you, my people
I say, your minds refresh!

Our grains have lost their purple
Our lands're drained to trash
Our hope has been a cripple.

Oh Vultures of our area,
The Cock has spread your vow
To maim what remains of Nigeria.

Listen to the Parrot now!
Even if you wake up earlier,
Tomorrow will end your prow.

Kuzo,

Let's Talk

Hausa, Yoruba

Kuzo

Kuzo 'yan uwa kuzo
Kuzo ga wakar Manzo
Mun yi murna zuwar Manzo
'Dan Abdullahi da rahma ya izo
Ya bakkomu alheri don darajan Manzo
Ga Kur'an, da hadisin Manzo
Ya ce in mún biyo a kurdus mùn izo
Amma fa sai da huswan Manzo
Al-Amin, rasulun Allah da ya izo

Kunnen ku nawa 'yan Nijeriya,
Shukabanin mun sunƙi su bi halin Manzo
Duk sun hana alhakin ɗan maraya
Shaƙiyyun, bari ganin sunan su kamar mabiyin Manzo
Ko kaɗan, ɗan iska duk sun rasa biyayya
Ai ka ga sun ɓata kasar nan da mun izo.
Shehu Usumanu da Audullahi na Gwandu sun yi
        wa'asiyya
Sun bar muna littafai da sunar Manzo
Kowabi in-sha-Allahu daɗi kam bai rasa,
Don biyayyar ga hadasa Manzo.
Ya Allah gafarce mu don darajar Manzo,
Dan Audullahi da ya izo.

Ijapa Tíroko (Waka)

Eyin ara mi, e wa gbó
Eyin ore mi, e wa gbó
Egb'orin owe to wu etii gbo
E gbo orin owe t'owo eti ninu
Orin Ijapa p'el'ogbo ewe re
E gboo orin owe to wo eti ninu.

Se'sa ti mo'japa pelu ogbo ewe
Ijapa tiroko oko Yonnibo,
T'oloruko ohun ni "Gbogboyin,"
Gbogbo eni t'oku k'osi ma je "Iwo,"
E ni ti k'oje "Iwo" a si ma je "Emi,"
Gbogbo onje ini ti gbogboyin,
Gbogbo aso ebi ti gbogbo ara,
Gbogbo ikan ini ti gbogbo ilu,
Gbogbo eronja ti'nu omi,
Gbogbo eronja t'inu ile,
Gbogbo dukiya t'oje ti jamaa,
Gbogbo re ni'japaa lo fowo re tan.

Se'sa ti mon'japaa ti mo ti n wi
Abi éè mo'japaa baba ti n da'gi?
To da'gi ni'lee, to da'gi l'oko
To da gi ebi, to tun da'gi ara,

To da'gi Saki, to da ni Lokoja,
Gogbo igi igbo ti di dida,
O da'gi Afonja, o da'gi Ake,
Gbogbo ilu lo da kodoro.
Baba n dagii, igida,
Layi Ko'pe ojo oko Yonnibo,
Bi gbogbo Abata aye ba fi e pamo,
Awon Abata orun a wu e jade.

Sakkwato, Birnin Shehu

Da sallama na bakkoku wannan tawwada,
'Dan ilori gida kowa na Allah.

Hii, duk mun san da haka,
Sakkwato, Birnin Shehu.
Da gida har zuwa daji,
gari dut zuwa ƙauye,
Ta Shehu, daraja Fodiye.

Da zuwar sa aka samu
haske ta ɓullo daga gabas,
Shehu ya biyo dukka ya saƙa muna,
Denge har zuwa Daura,
Har Bidda banufe,
haske ta ɓullo daka gabas,
Allahu Akbar, mun yi ruku'u
Sallah, ta gidan Fodiye.

Au, in ka san da haka,
Ka yi godiyar ga Allah.
Ka ji Bello Fodiye,
Sarkin musulumi mai babban kalam
Ya rubuto wakar adini,
Ya ce muyi sallah ko acikin ruwa muke.

Ko da yake tsohuwa takan karya a ranar asumi,
Dolle tsohuwa ta yi sallah in sallah ta ke.

Abubakar Siddiku na uku,
Yace yara insu kai shekaru bakwai,
Har masalaci mu kai su,
In sun kai shekara goma da ɗaya,
Da duk sun ƙi sallah kada mu ƙi bulala,
Ka ga bulala ita ce allan Yaro.
Ya Allahu, ya Allah,
Duk yaran mu kasa su bi wannan hayan,
ta Mustafa ɗan Amina.

Idan kana shakka wa ya kallami wannan waƙar
Ta Sakkwato birnin Shehu,
Nine Audu al-Rashid kowa na Allah,
Basakkwace dan Ilori!

Odolaye

(For legendary Odolaye Aremu, the late Ilorin Oral
Singer)

> *Odolaye Aremu, alalaye Ilorin,*
> *Akomo logbon Aremu, olohun-iyo oyin,*
> *Oloselu Aremu, oni waasu orin.*

Bee na ni, Odolaye olorin.
Odo laaye oo, Oluwa maje kodo o gbe wa lo.
Aremu oba ninu olorin,
Akorin bi eni jeko, alulu bi eni f'wo s'omi.

> *Odolaye Aremu, alalaye Ilorin,*
> *Akomo logbon Aremu, olohun-iyo oyin,*
> *Oloselu Aremu, oni waasu orin.*

Bee naa ni, Odolaye loo o,
Agbe rele a r'aro da mo
Aluko lo a rosun fi para,
Odolaye loo oo,
Ololufe Ilorin loo o,
Omo oko Ilorin loo oo,
Aja kwara ti kíí dun l'asan,
Bi ko ba r'eran asi r'eyan gbagudu.

Odolaye Aremu, alalaye Ilorin,
Akomo logbon Aremu, olohuniyo oyin,
Oloselu Aremu, oni waasu orin.

Bee na ni, Fitila Ilorin ti n tan yan,
Fitila na o ni ku l'aye l'aye.
Nijowo naa ni, Omoekere olorin lo!
Nijowo naa ni, Amao f'ile bo'ra bi aso,
Omoeke Amao garu olorin Ilorin.

Odolaye Aremu, alalaye Ilorin,
Akomo logbon Aremu, olohuniyo oyin,
Oloselu Aremu, oni waasu orin.

Bee na ni, Fitila Ilorin ti n tan yan,
Fitila na o ni ku l'aye l'aye.
Nijowo naa ni, erujeje Kinihun a da seriya f'erin aditi,
Sulu Gambari oko Sefi-Igbaja da'le bora bi aso.
Nijowo naa ni, AbdulKadiri dogo oni suru,
Nijowo naa lo p'eyinda!
Serikin goma, sammani goma!

Olohun ko f'erijoba,
Allahu Ko f'eri j'arole Alimi to p'eyinda,
Olohun ko f'erijoba.

Bee na ni, fitila Ilorin ti n tan yan,
Fitila na o ni ku l'aye l'aye.
Nijowo naa ni, Aafa Bábá Oba,
Adam Abdullahi f'ile bora bi aso;
Shehu Adama!

> *Iba se pe aeku laye o, aba ba Muhammadu*
> *Aba ba Muhammada,*
> *Oke mefa l'egbaji, awa o ba kan ma l'aye.*
> *Toreta ti Musa o,*
> *Injila fun Isa*
> *Seburatu Dawuda,*
> *Alukurani f'onsenla.*

Bee na ni ololufe Ilorin.
Oluwa k'oforijolorin,
Lola iluu Ilorin,
Ilorin Afonja enu dun b'iyo.
Ilu to bi toyi o leegun rara,
Esin leegun Ile wa,
Oko l'oro be.
Arikewu s'ola, afi walaa t'ore.
Odolaye Olorin, o ni "Kosibi t'olohun o si,
Ama Ilorin ni n sun."

> *Odolaye Aremu, alalaye Ilorin,*
> *Akomo l'ogbon Aremu, olohun-iyo oyin,*
> *Oloselu Aremu, oni waasu orin.*

Atibàbà yi mama tîî lo,
Igi gendu yii mama tîî lo,
Arole Afonja mama tîî lo,
Iyesi Alimi mama tîî lo,
Olohun ko lora emin faari Ilorin gbogbo,
Aafaa agba, Muhammadu Kamaluddini!
Oloyè, Oloyé, Aafa baboba, magaji, akowe,
Omokewu,
Olorin awureebe, Oniwaka, Dadakuada, Onibalu,
Eyin iyè Ilorin, ema ko lorin:
Oluwa ni ngbeniga.

> *Odolaye Aremu, alalaye Ilorin,*
> *Akomo l'ogbon Aremu, olohun-iyo oyin,*
> *Oloselu Aremu, oni waasu orin.*

Se bee na ni?
Loju gbogbo wa ni Ilorin,
Ki l'eye kowe n se ti kole k'orin?
Fasiti Ilorin, ki l'eye kowe n se ti kole k'orin?
Ijoba kwara, ki l'eye kowe n se ti kole k'orin?
Naijiriya, ki l'eye kowe n se ti kole k'orin?!
Ki l'anfani fasiti ti o le siti!

> *Odolaye Aremu, alalaye Ilorin,*
> *Akomo logbon Aremu, olohun-iyo oyin,*
> *Oloselu Aremu, oni waasu orin.*

Fasiti Ilorin, ki l'anfani fasiti ti ko le si'ni l'eti!
Adama Abdullahi Ilorin, aafa gbogbo aye, fasiti ki
     l'ese?
Ile aafa alimi, alubarika gbogbo aye, fasiti ki l'ese?
Aafa Agba k'emi yin ogun, akewu-kewe Ilorin, fasiti
     ki l'ese?
Bàba agba, Woli Olohun arole Alimi, Abudulikadiri:
     Seehu; fasiti ki l'ese?!
Odolaye Aremu Baba oselu olorin, ó l'oro Ilorin ò
     l'eja n bakan n nún, fasiti ki l'ese?
Amàá-kòkò n be labayawo, igba n be ni masingba,
     abata n be l'adabata, fasiti ki l'ese?
Aso-Oke n be l'okemale, ileke n be l'asinleke, emi nbe
l'abemi fasiti ki
     le se?
Eye kowe to ti sùn ko ji,
Ilorin l'asà, a l'olohun!

> *Ilorin Afonja, so ni ki wa ni?*
> *Ab'oma wa, o ni ki wa ni?*

Ilorin Afonja, o ni ki wa ni?
Ab'oma wa, o ni ki wa ni?

> *Ilorin Afonja, so ni ki wa ni?*
> *Ab'oma wa, o ni ki wa ni?*

96

Tributes, Hopes, Life

Bílíkísu

The moon and the sun
beckon to the earth
Pleading for her fruits of life.
Bilikisu, you are those fruits:
Earth, fruits of earth!

Bilikisu, my earth, mother earth,
Earth to sun and moon and stars
Mother earth,
Earth to water and sand
Earth mother, Olomoyoyo[1].

Earth,
Today I celebrate your names
Which I learnt to pronounce from birth
Your many names:
Poles affirming your boat that floats freely
    on the ocean.

---

1 Mother of many children; always in the midst of children.

Your names, mother,
Are the stars
Shinning on your clean wrappers
Unsoiled by the oily palmoil sheet
That soak all clothes around.
Mother earth,
The unbending path to the course
 of amuye—drink-and-survive spring,
mother,
is your name.
Your words, constant and changeless,
Always come to pass.

Mother,
Yet you shed tears
of labor and torture.
Tears,
of deprivation and poverty.
Tears,
of the war of the
inner caucus of the
household caucu-ses.
Tears,
of the war of the younger
one
Who learns to mount her hands on the elder
And hit you in threes and fours.

100

Mother,
Your wails shall soon be smiles
Your names shall bear you out!
Ọlọmọyọyọ,
You shall earn
Your hearty yearns:
Peace, justice, progress and
Comfort.
Soon, mother.

Oyinbo 'Lee Waa

(for Professor David Cook)

> *Oyinbo 'lee waa*
> *Oyinbo 'lee waa*
> *O n 'jẹ tuwo, o n jẹ kọọ yangan.*

Awoko bird is here,
Awoko of the sonorous voice,
Whoever hears my art
Offers banana and palm oil
to appease my might.

> *Oyinbo 'lee waa*
> *Oyinbo 'lee waa...*

Fellows in the cult;
Awoko,
King of birds,
I come as I do:
The lion appears
And the forest trembles in fear:
Will you or will you not
Chorus my songs?

Oyinbo 'lee waa
Oyinbo 'lee waa…

I say, partners in the cult,
The sun today
Dims its light,
The alogogo-igba
Gongs his message:
Oyinbo 'le wa
Steps the right foot
Out
Bẹmbẹ feast
Booms in the palace.

Oyinbo 'lee waa
Oyinbo 'lee waa…

Defidi is the spring
Assuaging our thirst;
He who has never seen another's farm
Claims his father's as the largest.

Oyinbo 'lee waa
Oyinbo 'lee waa…

Odiḍẹrẹ traverses the space,
Travels north, travels south,
But never fails to fly back.
Defidi, Oyinbo,
The sun rises in the morning,
Returns at night to bed;
however long in the sea
Home must you return, Oyinbo.

> *Oyinbo 'lee waa*
> *Oyinbo 'lee waa...*

Gunugun never dies young.
Defidi, Oyinbo,
Death is expelled from your eyes,
Disease is dismissed from your head;
Your eyes shall age
As the world ages.

> *Oyinbo 'lee waa*
> *Oyinbo 'lee waa...*

When you put your other leg
On the land of snow,
Echo, elegant voice:
To Africa I have been,
And Africa I have seen.

Oyinbo 'lee waa
Oyinbo 'lee waa...

Oyinbo 'lee waa
Breakfasts on ẹko-yangan;
Lunches on amala;
For a feast of pounded yam
Treks a hundred miles.
Oyinbo 'lee waa!

Iyapopo Odee

Iyapopo Odee oo
Saara Odee oo
Omoluabi Odee oo
Saara Odee oo ho

Ashes assuming the face of a dying fire,
Offsprings assuming the abode of their lineages.
Odee baby-mother,
When mother passes beyond, mother does remain.

Iyapopo Odee oo
Saara Odee oo
Omoluabi Odee oo
Saara Odee oo ho

Odee
I feel your touch
As my umbilical cord severs from my mother's womb
I feel your warmth as I cry
from the severance from my peaceful abode
to this laborious site
your touch pets me
smiles at me

Whispers:
Peace,
welcome
t' this abode of a Fitting Path.
Saraa taught me that day to remain a favorer of
    the lineage.
She called me: lover of the Guider to
the house of my ancestors.

Iyapopo Odee oo
Saara Odee oo
Omoluabi Odee oo
Saara Odee oo ho

As your glittering eyes dim their light
one afternoon, I knew
you only rested, and would wake up again.

Iyapopo Odee oo
Saara Odee oo
Omoluabi Odee oo
Saara Odee oo ho

Here, your eyes shine afresh and
bring light, illuminating
the corners of our happiness.

Iyapopo Odee oo
Saara Odee oo
Omoluabi Odee oo
Saara Odee oo ho

Oh Saara,
what a day in the world you arrived.
On my arms, Asabi, your distinct-birth.
I touched you, and in your ears,
Whispered:
Welcome
Witness this
Peace.
Iyapopo, cloths, the clothes of my being.

Iyapopo Odee oo
Saara Odee oo
Omoluabi Odee oo
Saara Odee oo ho.

Kokewu-kobere

Kokewu kobere, yo ti se mọ oo
Kokewu kobere, yo ti se mọ oo

I heard your song in the equidistant of night
I heard
and woke up
to enlist in your army,
Kokewu-Kobere, Soldier in the battle of our minds.

Kokewu kobere, yo ti se mọ oo
Kokewu kobere, yo ti se mọ oo

Your bullet words pearced deaf ears
and sent them early to the sandy rivers
    of their souls
Your songs had taste to them,
Those who heard couldn't return to sleep
But went out to shed away their garments of darkness
    and wore turbans befitting the household of Alimi.

Kokewu kobere, yo ti se mọ oo
Kokewu kobere, yo ti se mọ oo

Kokewu-Kobere, your songs
taught us to cleanse our souls
    and body
in readiness for the market day.
Some thought all we needed were cowries,
filling pockets of our cloths.
You said we needed
cleanliness
to attract buyers in the market.
Kokewu, your wisdom today lights up the moon of our
    emporium.

Kokewu kobere, yo ti se mọ oo
Kokewu kobere, yo ti se mọ oo

Kokewu-Kobere,
When a child cuts a tree from beneath, an elder knows
    indeed where it'll fall.
Cowrieneers, despite their gold and diamonds
Despite their shops filled up with Washington washers
Despite the glossiness of their houses rugged with
imported sands from Arabia,
Today's market is ours!
Customers run away from the odour of their decaying
    sore,
Customers cannot stand the lice of their untouched
    hair!

Kokewu kobere, yo ti se mọ oo
Kokewu kobere, yo ti se mọ oo

Our *Ofi*, our *Alaari*
win customers for us in the market.
Kokewu-Kobere, your impeccable lessons
    win for our souls
the brightness of the sky before the moon goes to bed.
It gives us the glory
of the morning as it wakes up from its sleep.
What a brilliant day
    in Alimi's city!

Kokewu kobere, yo ti se mọ oo
Kokewu kobere, yo ti se mọ oo

Kokewu-Kobere, we still sing your song,
Kokewu kobere, yo ti se mọ oo
Kokewu kobere, yo ti se mọ oo
So sweet we eat't as we eat *tuwo*
We drink it as we drink *ẹkọ-gbona*,
It's the secret for the brightness of the Ilorin Sky.

Kokewu kobere, yo ti se mọ oo
Kokewu kobere, yo ti se mọ oo

Ajongolo

(For Ajongolo, Kokewu-Kobere, Salman-Ake, Kamal,
Adam, Yahaya, Salihu, Sallah, Iyakewu, AbdulRaheem,
others, born, unborn.)

The stars in our sky
Boom enough light to
exhilarate the sky;
The moon in our bucket
Gives strong buoyancy,
stirs the bucket water
with illuminating grace.

How will the sky look without the stars?
How would our water smell
without the powerful alum of the refining moon!
What food will grow without the rays of our soothing
    sun!
How would our bones feel,
without the massaging touch of the sun's hands, how?

Without these stars Ilorin sky would be dark,
Without them who boom lights to our earth,
no one would detect cotton in Ilorin night,
no one would have eyes to sew clothes,
without inserting needles into his/her fingers.

When Ajọngọlọ reached Ode-alausa,
and looked askance at the sky,
he sang with the words unknown to ears,
before his eyes returned to the ground,
rain rained all through our land,
leaving us water to drink forever.

Masire, the Listening Lion

However sweet kolanut gets in the mouth,
it disappears after moments of chewing.
However delicious *dabidun*[1] is,
only its meat reaches the stomach,
its seed returns back to the soil.
Masire, only a few lions in the forest
Have patience to listen to the whimper
    of their own shadows:
However strong the wish to chew meat for long in the
    mouth,
the pull of the throat won't allow it to stay.

Ketumile,
If Leopard had ears for the gorge,
it wouldn't be a prey for Tiger.
If fishes had eyes to see hungry Whales in the sea,
their bones wouldn't end up crushed
under the molars of the Whale.

Tell me Masire,
how did the farmer

---

1 *Dabidun* is a sweet crop called "dates", found in
  Arabia, and popular in Northern Nigeria.

Know his cutlass so well that it cuts grasses,
not his hands!
What deals did the farmer make with hoe,

For the hoe to have spared his legs?
Tell me Katumile,
Why did cat dance so well,
while frog only jumped
like one whose legs were tied up with string!

Katumile,
If all hunters would take heed of the sun when it goes
    down in the forest,
and return home like you,
Mwalimu,
If hunting dogs would hear their masters' whistle,
and come home before forest ghosts prepare for their
    feast,
Kaunda, Senghor,
If only flies would leave honey pots
    after taking their bellies' shares,
More pots of honey would remain
devoid of the contamination of the flies!
Forest ghosts would dance and have only ghosts to eat.
Our sun would go high in the sky,
and send it rays
to every corner of our homes.

Mandela

When I saw that you had a cap on your head, Mandela,
I inquired about its texture secretly of its weaver.
Secretly, she told me,
that your cap wasn't made of cloth,
it wasn't a cap of iron,
it wasn't a cap of diamonds of the mines.
She told me
that your cap was of a texture only you
could tell,
You, Mandela, made the material of your cap;
You, alone, know its texture.

How'd you say, thanks?

How'd you express gratitude,
when a fleshy tide raises your latitude,
in a moony circle of lovely fluid?
How'd you say, thanks?

Ask her who has the
delicate water in her veins,
flowing in the riverbed
of sunny strips.
Ask her where this laughter
raining from her heart
comes from,
then you'll know how
You'll say, thanks.

Queen Amina

Our own woman of fame
Our Queen of Zazzau
woman warrior,
stinged like scorpion on battle fronts.

Amina, I heard the news
of your mighty sword,
how it cut enemies's necks to the ground.
I heard how brave men urinated in their pants
on seeing the standing muscles of your arms.
Some stumbled on your shadow
and ran helter-skelter to the bush, falling
deep into the ditch you dug the night before.

Amina, you're no ornamental casserole in the castle,
or an efflorescence shifted from palace to palace.
You're a warrior on battle fronts,
ruler that made the rules,
authority that authorized men to walk free on the
    street or
lock themselves up in the hovel of their backyards.

Our Queen of Zazzau,
I saw the bulwarks around the borders of your nations.
In Birnin Yauri, your sage symbols

on sands, on leaves, on trees
I saw your history on people's faces,
I heard drummers beat patterns in your praise-names,
I saw singers reenact your schematic steps on war
    fields.
Amina, I grew up chanting your heroic poetry.

Our Queen of Zazzau
I dreamt,
my little Tigress grew up having
a poetry as cool as yours;
even cooler!
Hungry animals
ate with her in the same bowls,
laughed from the joy of their common freedom,
chorused her praise-names as the new Amina.

Lioness of Zazzau,
Many animals take pride,
learning
your name
anew.

Tutuola, mutuwa dole

(no drum or music of any kind)

> *Idan mutuwa ta sallama[1]*
> *Aguje sai ka amsa*
> *Ko giwa adaji*
> *da gudu yaje akhira*
> *Tutuola, mutuwa dole*

Tutuola, my eyes
sight see sides of your changing cloud.
Oh, Hamattan wind
steer this song of *sallama*[2]

---

1 The refrain, in Hausa, translates thus: "When death
   comes knocking/With speed you (find yourself)
   answering/Even Elephant in the forest/Ran to answer
   its call/Tutuola, death a must!" This poem is written
   for the late Nigerian writer, Amos Tutuola.

2 Some of the non-English words, mostly in Hausa lan-
   guage, used in this poem include: *sallama*, farewell;
   kalangu, talking drum; *Garin Alimi*, Alimi town;
   bembe, a kind of Yoruba drum; *kalam*, an Arabic word
   adopted in Hausa to mean "pen" or what has been
   written. Also *sallama* is originally from Arabic/Islamic
   word, *salam*, "peace, hello."

This *kalangu*, his
From a crowing cock of *Garin Alimi*.

>*Idan mutuwa ta sallama*
>*Aguje sai ka amsa*
>*Ko giwa adaji*
>*da gudu yaje akhira*
>*Tutuola, mutuwa dole*

Tutuola, you drew your ink from this ocean
This ocean, flowing across our land
You drew your words from the bottom
    of our cultural ocean, flowing,
Forming new waters that fertilized the soil of our
    farming,
and brought trees of palm
with kernels so much close like a collection of
    broomsticks.

>*Idan mutuwa ta sallama*
>*Aguje sai ka amsa*
>*Ko giwa adaji*
>*da gudu yaje akhira*
>*Tutuola, mutuwa dole*

Tutuola, your tapers
climbed without the cord

They tapped your trees and drank the sour wine
A strange wine they knew not,
They drank the fresh sweetness
and climbed to tap for more.

> *Idan mutuwa ta sallama*
> *Aguje sai ka amsa*
> *Ko giwa adaji*
> *da gudu yaje akhira*
> *Tutuola, mutuwa dole*

Tutuola, your wine of cultural corn
wet many hungry mouths,
assuaged the thirst for African meal.
The dances abroad,
brought your *bembe* drum alive.
They learned to dance to
a rhythm so strange, so sweet.

> *Idan mutuwa ta sallama*
> *Aguje sai ka amsa*
> *Ko giwa adaji*
> *da gudu yaje akhira*
> *Tutuola, mutuwa dole*

Tutuola, your fertility wine
dimmed no eyes!

Your wine brightened
Minds of your peers,
and set free their skeptical hearts
From the fear of drunkenness.

> *Idan mutuwa ta sallama*
> *Aguje sai ka amsa*
> *Ko giwa adaji*
> *da gudu yaje akhira*
> *Tutuola, mutuwa dole*

Tutuola, the song is still loud
    after your journey.
Your peers have joined in the celebration
of these oceans you brought home,
they danced, and drank,
to the waters that flow from the course of your spring.

> *Idan mutuwa ta sallama*
> *Aguje sai ka amsa*
> *Ko giwa adaji*
> *da gudu yaje akhira*
> *Tutuola, mutuwa dole*

Tutuola, what a season for your singing bird to leave
    our forest!
What a season to depart

the crude plane of Nigerian bushes.
No, your flying bird does well to fly out,
Else these hunters of our *daji*—forest
Would strip off your eyes for soup.

> *Idan mutuwa ta sallama*
> *Aguje sai ka amsa*
> *Ko giwa adaji*
> *da gudu yaje akhira*
> *Tutuola, mutuwa dole*

Tutuola, how
could your feathers remain mute, when the
   kalam is dry,
When Mighty Wind
Called for a greater feast for you!
Fly, Tutuola, fly
Fly as far as your feathers can go!
Sometime, our birds will fly on with you.

> *Idan mutuwa ta sallama*
> *Aguje sai ka amsa*
> *Ko giwa adaji*
> *da gudu yaje akhira*
> *Tutuola, mutuwa dole*

When Rain Falls

(better performed with *Kalangu*[1] musical accompaniment)

(For C. Bouygues, and all Teachers of African Cultures)

> In ruwan sama ya faɗo, ya jike ƙasa
> Ya taru a rijiya, a samu na sha

When rain falls
The earth is enriched
Our wells are full
Our throats are wet.

> In ruwan sama ya faɗo, ya jike ƙasa
> Ya taru a rijiya, a samu na sha

When the cloud gathers, ripens
 chooses a wisdom farm
To precipitate its water.

---

1 *Kalangu* is a traditional Hausa drum. Its music will provide this poem with a traditional Hausa flavor. The refrain, written in Hausa, is translated into English in the second stanza.

In ruwan sama ya faɗo...

Such water never tires, never dies
Flows north,
Flows south.

In ruwan sama ya faɗo, ...

Such water,
Colorless, tasteless
Pure, bright
Showers its light on all corners of the globe

In ruwan sama ya faɗo, ...

We all in this fountain
Are waters of life,
Waters of fertility.
 Our mangoes, our oranges
 Our pineapples and papaws
 Are food for all.

In ruwan sama ya faɗo, ...

Claude,
Your retiring water,
Will never tire.

It'll reach out to desert farms,
And feed other trees
Long after your Kuka-tree[2]
Ceases to live.

> In ruwan sama ya faɗo, ya jike ƙasa
> Ya taru a rijiya, a samu na sha

---

2 *Kuka* is a Hausa name for a kind of tree whose leaves
   are used in making a type of soup, *Miyan kuka*.

Day Break,

Laughter,

Love

A Sun of our Earth

Alihamudu o yẹ ka dupẹ o
Alhamudu o yẹ ka dupẹ
Alhamudu o yẹ ka dupẹ o
Alhamudu o yẹ ka dupẹ
B'ẹru dupe ore a si gbamiran
Alhamdu o yẹ ka dupẹ.

Okoto-the snail shell has been celebrated as a great
    dancer
Insects, as dancers to ride an open air dancing to the
    rhythm of invisible music.
Neither snail nor insects can surpass my dancing steps
    today
The *bushra*[1] of your crown, Obaabu[2] , is a mighty sun of
    our earth.

---

1 An Arabic word for good news. There's a program
   every Friday on Radio Kwara Ilorin, Nigeria, called
   "Bushra" produced by Alhaji Adebayo Sallah.

2 This poem is dedicated to Oba AbdulRaheem
   (Popularly called 'Obaabu' by Ilorin youths),
   Professor of English, and newly elected Vice-
   Chancellor of the University of Ilorin in Nigeria; the
   first Ilorin indigine to hold such a position in Nigeria.
   This poem was originally started as a tribute to him
   when he became a full professor of English at Bayero
   University, Kano.

Alihamudu o yẹ ka dupẹ o
Alihamudu o yẹ ka dupẹ
Alihamudu o yẹ ka dupẹ o
Alihamudu o yẹ ka dupẹ
B'ẹru dupẹ ore a si gbamiran
Alihamudu o yẹ ka dupẹ.

Whoever dances than me today
must prepare to show a body farther than Jupiter in
    the galaxy,
Must wear diamond shoes and dance to the
    bottomless of the earth
While still floating on the surface of a slippery pond;
Must have mouths as salty as those of the offspring of
    Afonja;
Must be Jimba in the palace of Ilorin!
Whoever wants to surpass me today
Must extol: Seeuu,
and raise his fist in homage
to our Ọba, the doyen of Ilorin.

Alihamudu o yẹ ka dupẹ o
Alihamudu o yẹ ka dupẹ
Alihamudu o yẹ ka dupẹ o
Alihamudu o yẹ ka dupẹ
B'ẹru dupẹ ore a si gbamiran
Alihamudu o yẹ ka dupẹ.

That day
when others rushed to dig for money
    to take to market,
Ilorin opted to know the taste of the water
    under the rock
It opted to know who spread the massive carpet
    above our atmosphere
and yet allowed the sun's rays to visit
    searchingly on the ground.
Ilorin, thou had no *nairabags*, but
Thou hath the telescope to search
    into the heart of the earth
where waters hid their faces.
Thou hath access beneath the rock,
and dreweth water for ablution.

Alihamudu o yẹ ka dupẹ o
Alihamudu o yẹ ka dupẹ
Alihamudu o yẹ ka dupẹ o
Alihamudu o yẹ ka dupẹ
B'ẹru dupẹ ore a si gbamiran
Alihamudu o yẹ ka dupẹ.

Drink, Ilorin, drink
Drink, Abdulkadiri, drink
Drink, Ọba, drink your delectable water,
And cleanse the soil of sorely particles.

Share your water with thirsty souls
whose mouths remained open for ages.

Alihamudu o yẹ ka dupẹ o
Alihamudu o yẹ ka dupẹ
Alihamudu o yẹ ka dupẹ o
Alihamudu o yẹ ka dupẹ
B'ẹru dupẹ ore a si gbamiran
Alihamudu o yẹ ka dupẹ.

Obaabu, sing *maadalla*, with all your mouth.
Join in singing the waka of Labeka
Chorus, the sky is only
a beginning.

Alihamudu o yẹ ka dupẹ o
Alihamudu o yẹ ka dupẹ
Alihamudu o yẹ ka dupẹ o
Alihamudu o yẹ ka dupẹ
B'ẹru dupẹ ore a si gbamiran
Alihamudu o yẹ ka dupẹ.

Edmonton

Three Suns have passed
since I landed on this tin,
I came to the wedge of the town.
First, a field of cotton!
No, a field of salt!!
What else can be as white as
A cotton mass mounted by cotton
A site still strange in croton.

Alas, a stranger still, I'd been bitten
Oh I have been beaten!
A tropical Gala came to town!
Cotton snowball'n Edmonton.
Poor boy of the tropical cotton
Snow t'him's another cotton,
Edmonton snow is cotton,
only it's made of water.

Soon I ran up to Eaton's,
and got myself some Etons.
What a blowing blue Eton,
In Strathcona Orpington.
Oh, to a runner skeleton,
Or to a fatter motton,
all the pull of Triton.

Oh oily Triton,
it's your double-smarter city:
a smarter whiter snowy
on a smarter blacker goldy!
A smatter citadel-Alberta,
the smarter magician of triton:
a commander of proton,
the smither of neutron,
Oh Edmonton Alberta!!

Before I Run Real Crazy

These soft layers in the sky,
blue-ing, booming,
charming,
cooling, awaking
all hairs in my body cells,
opening out my head locks ,
feverishing my eyes,
sweep me into a moody salivation for the
    sweetness of your paradise.
Oh I'm, I'm lost in this elastic sensation of
    an approaching ecstasy.
Oh, p-l-e-a-s-e Kraaaama, Oh!
You must come over now before I
RUN REAL CRAZY

Wonder Cook

My tongue peeps
    to see what magnet so powerful
    to see what magic pulls it out so.

My mouth wonders wide,
    "What salivating tide
    causes my saliva to fill this bucket?"

Alas, One Magic Cook
    it is. My tongue hooked
    My mouth helpless at
    the witchery of her *sewu*[1] aroma

Oh Wonder Cook
Allow my mouth the elysium
    of your aromatic meal.

---

1 A Korean word for shrubs.

How Close?

How fast would a pathfinder fly to celebrate its feat of
    reaching the mars?
How beautiful would a magnet get to be proud of
    attracting iron plates unto its body?
How big would a plane be to fly from Lagos to Kano?

Karamah, how close to you must your heart be,
before you feel its laughter and excitement
for being housed in your chest?
How frequently do you want your eyelids to twinkle,
before you know that they celebrate the chance to
    serve your eyes?

Your lioness may be meek
about the thickness of her own skin,
but the lion knows the forest well,
He knows well the forest,
and celebrates his luck of resting under the lioness's
    hide.

Afterword

Can The Finger Stop
The Train

With a nodding acknowledgement to Canada, the place of origin of this collection of poems, one might feel like asking, to change Wiebe but slightly, whom is the voice intended for. Alas, in all probability, this does not constitute a valid question anymore, in these times of incessantly fragmented selves, in these times of constant global stretching, where one is torn asunder between the IMF's harsh conditionality, the stupendous profits of a handful of global players and the budgets of nations being balanced by the broken backs of their poor.

Sitting on the fence so-to-speak, with one toe in the ground of Alberta, and more than a full leg in the soil of Ilorin, the poet gives way to "the urge to write", as Ofeimun put it way back in the Eighties in his "Time for Tongue to Flower". In his own words, the poet now knows "how low our roof has come".

He is eager to take sides in the Chinweizu sense and protests a non-elitist stance. With *Kalangu* accompaniment emphasis is laid on the performance angle, and, more often than not, conventional aesthetics are upturned. With his head in the clouds of issues, the poet's heart and shoulder sink probing shafts in the local community. A syncretism of sorts is programmatic, with a language mix of English, Hausa and Yoruba (and the exceptional

Pidgin), and the occasional comprehensive gesture across the national boarders of Nigeria.

He invokes the beggar tradition of the Wolof in the vein of Ousmane and Sow Fall. Yet he does not really spit at the fallen mighty, as the rural beggars do in *Xala*, to scourge the corruption of the urban elite. The social position of the outsider congeals into the point-of-view of the underdog. Yet an excess of specificity is avoided and the appeal is generalized as becomes evident in the many annotations which are obviously addressed to the non-Nigerian monoglot reader.

The poet's voice strives after the freshness and immediacy of youth and the reader might often have a feeling not dissimilar from the experience of old Deeriye in Farah's *Close Sesame* when he seeks to sympathize with the secret undertakings of his son Mursal in the analysis of "the mad discourse of the sane". In the course of the collection, the initial quite abstract aloofness becomes more and more concrete, as the big issues give way to local impressions and incantations. Thus the tremors of East Timor can better be left to the likes of John Pilger, whereas Mandela's cap is sure to fascinate. The warmth of human touch is most clearly felt, when a very personal voice records encounters and conjures up dear memories.

The jarring tone of distorting alliterations does not always successfully convey the notions of disintegra-

144

tion and utmost discrepancy, but the global village of discordant reciprocity convincingly comes across in the phrase: "I rub your back, you cut mine to the bones."

Peter O. Stummer
Munich, Germany
March 15, 1998

Almajiri

The title of this volume of poems makes their intention—this is a volume about the dispossessed of the world in Africa. Its appeal is meant to be in Africa. The term of the title is understood widely in Africa and will be understood by anyone who chooses to read and contemplate the poems in English, Hausa-Fulani and Yoruba, the languages in which the poems are cast, sometime individually and sometimes mixing languages and dialects. The poet—a scholar who provides a useful but minimal scholarly apparatus to assist his readers—defines the implications of his title and explains his choice of languages. The term Almajiri is widely used in West Africa: it is widely interpreted in various cultures in West Africa. He is invariably poor, often blind but possessing the intuitive insights of the blind and the power of the griot to give expression to his understanding. He lists the places and countries where through which the almajiri range and the three languages in which are given the expression of his experiences.

Na'Allah writes in the local dialects of Hausa - Fulani and Yoruba. And he agrees with Chinua Achebe that dialects within major languages groups should not be tampered with, that the vitality of a language originates in its local idiosyncrasy, and that standardizing a language "kills literary and aesthetic identity [in] a work of art."

Some of the poems here are what might be called lyrics and some are occasional. But for the most part the poems are about the plight of the poor and dispossessed, statements moving between the overt and the implied, about the causes for the dispossession—the abnegation of leadership—and an assertion of the relentless will of the Almajiris to endure and prevail.

Almajiri is a volume in the tradition of poetry by Osundare, Ojaide, Garuba to mention but three contemporaries of Na'Allah. And apart from the perspective of these poets and the civilians whose lives their poems celebrate, many of Na'Allah's poems share with these poets the belief that the poems "come alive in public performance where their sociocultural and literary aesthetics are fully realized."

This is poetry of great power, fixed in the perspectives of the Almajiris, wide-ranging in the experience it conveys, widely allusive in its metaphorical base and protean and powerful in its linguistic appeal.

Douglas Killam
Guelph, Canada
March 20, 1998